W9-AMN-522

Incredibly Disgusting Drugs™

Abusing Prescription Drugs

Philip Wolny

New York

For my grandfather, Jan Hetlof

Published in 2008 by The Rosen Publishing Group, Inc.
29 East 21st Street, New York, NY 10010

First Edition

Library of Congress Cataloging-in-Publication Data

Wolny, Philip.
Abusing prescription drugs / Philip Wolny. — 1st ed.
p. cm. — (Incredibly disgusting drugs)
Includes bibliographical references and index.
ISBN-13: 978-1-4042-1955-7 (hardcover)
ISBN-10: 1-4042-1955-2 (hardcover)
1. Drug abuse—Juvenile literature. 2. Medication abuse—Juvenile literature.
3. Teenagers—Drug abuse—Juvenile literature. I. Title.
RC564.3.W65 2008
362.29—dc22

2007007566

Manufactured in China

Contents

Introduction

Eddie Cappello, of Brooklyn, New York, died in his bed from a drug overdose on February 17, 2005. He was only twenty-two years old, but he had a history of problems with legal and illegal drugs. Eddie had gone through drug abuse, then treatment, then relapse (a return to using drugs or alcohol) before his parents discovered him. He had hidden his drug use from his parents very well.

Many young people like Eddie have died from taking dangerous illegal substances—cocaine, heroin, or methamphetamine. But Eddie was part of a growing trend of deaths and serious problems caused by legal drugs that doctors and other medical specialists can provide to children as young as six years old. Eddie died not from coke or other illegal stimulants but from mixing too many pills of the prescription drug Xanax with an unidentified opiate, or narcotic drug.

Introduction

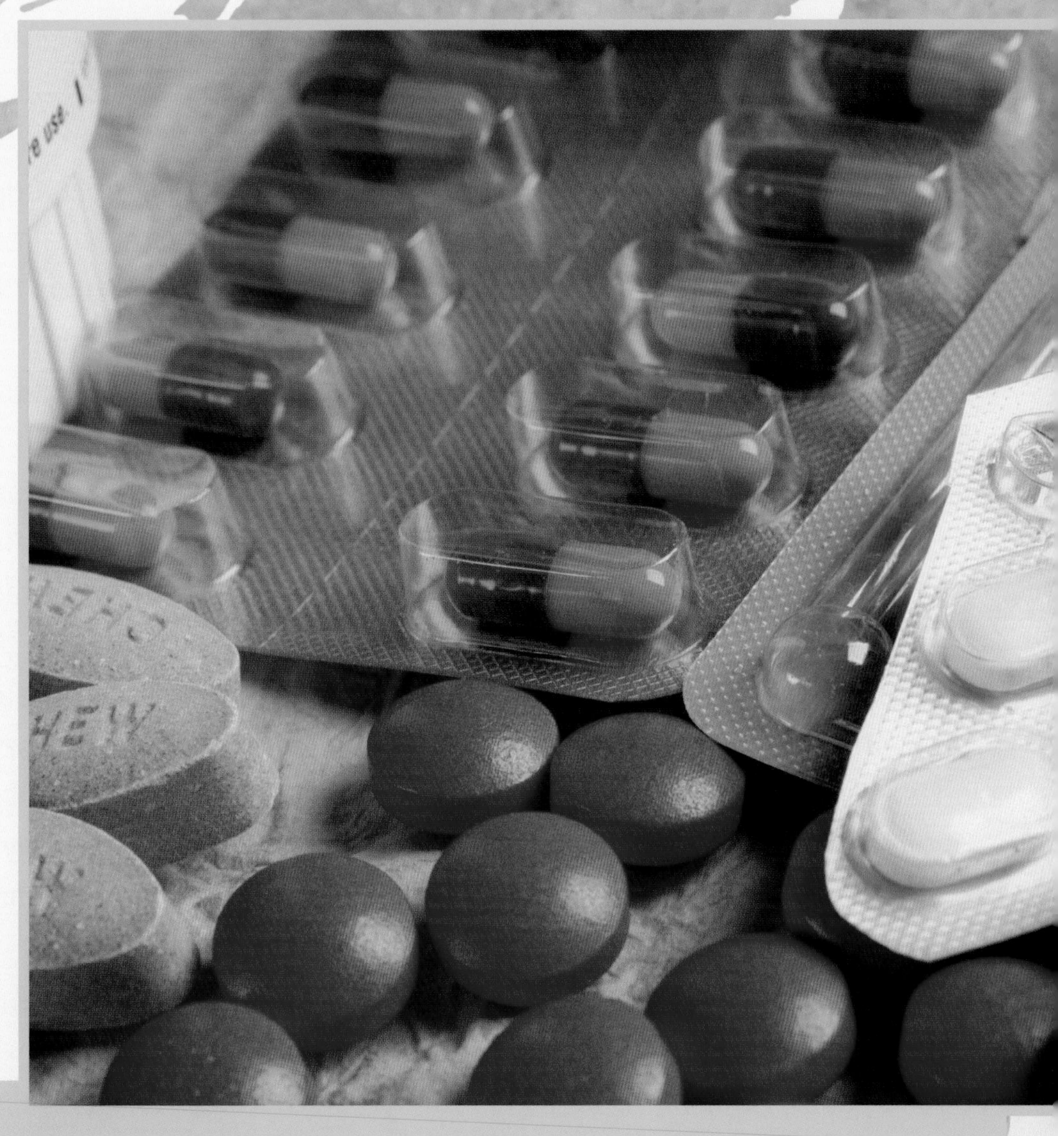

Prescription drugs make up a multibillion-dollar industry worldwide. The use of prescription drugs and the extent to which they are abused are greatly increasing.

Prescription drugs are used legally to help people with many illnesses and disorders. But the illegal use of prescription drugs is quickly becoming one of the biggest health crises in the United States. The *Journal of the American Medical Association* recently reported that prescription drug abuse is the fourth-leading cause of death in the United States, after heart disease, cancer, and stroke. Nobody is immune from prescription drug abuse, as it occurs in all social, economic, geographic, and ethnic groups.

When we think of drug abuse, we often think of illegal "street drugs" like cocaine or heroin. Everyone knows that users risk their health and even their lives by using these drugs to feel good or to escape from reality. Such drugs have no medical use. In recent years, however, people have taken to abusing drugs that are prescribed to help those with real mental and medical problems.

At the very least, prescription drug abusers are at risk for health problems. They also risk getting in trouble with the law because selling or possessing prescription drugs without a prescription is a crime. Abusers often feel irritable, restless, or not quite like themselves. They may also suffer from minor ailments ranging from increased heart rate to nausea and terrible mood swings. Or they may suffer from major problems brought on by changes in their brain and body chemistry. In some situations, prescription drug abuse can lead to death. Young people, whose bodies are developing rapidly, risk permanent damage to their health. What follows is the incredibly disgusting story of what prescription drugs can do to those who choose to abuse them.

1 What Is Prescription Drug Abuse?

What is a prescription drug? "Prescription drug" is a term used to distinguish a particular medicine from an over-the-counter (OTC) drug, which can be obtained without a prescription. Prescription drugs are regulated by law. A person who needs one of these drugs requires an official note, or prescription, from a licensed doctor in order to obtain and use it. Over the last few decades, Americans have turned to thousands of new prescription drugs to help them deal with physical and mental health problems. For better or for worse, these medications have become an accepted part of our society. Along with their legal use, however, has come an increase in their illegal or unregulated use. More and more people are using prescription medications for recreational use—as "party drugs," in other words. Others use prescription drugs to treat themselves, even though no doctor has prescribed them.

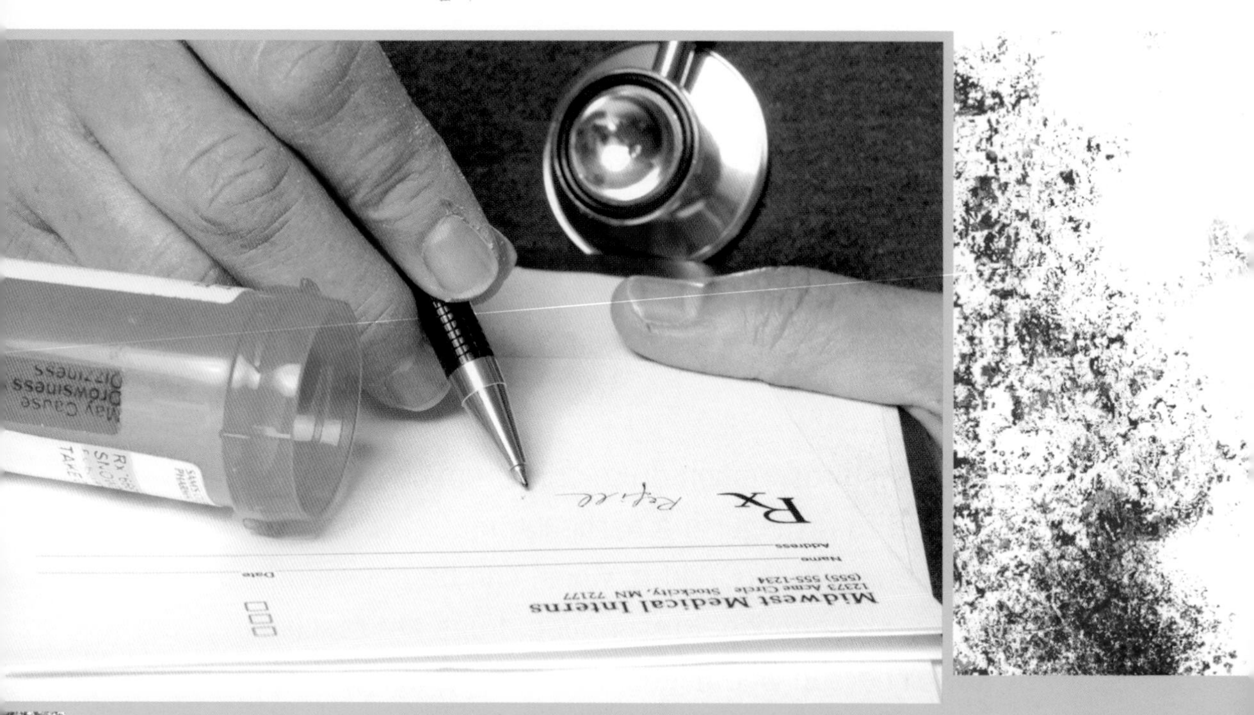

A written prescription is the standard document that doctors provide their patients so that they may legally obtain the drugs they need.

This tactic, commonly called self-medication, is also considered abuse. The increase in the illegal use of prescription drugs has caused an alarming rise in health problems and drug-related deaths.

Prescription Drugs as Party Drugs

Teens—and even preteens—in all parts of the United States now use an endless variety of prescription drugs as party drugs. With some pills, users take greater amounts than are recommended. Or they take them in ways that aren't intended. For example, they snort crushed-up pills, as one would snort cocaine or other powder drugs.

These young users take drugs for many reasons. Some just want to have fun, try something new, or fit in. They take prescription drugs because they like the feeling they get from them. This is the typical reason why people consume alcohol or smoke marijuana, too. Other users have trouble with depression or anxiety and take drugs to help them escape from their emotional problems. They get a good feeling, or rush, from taking drugs—at least for a while. The problem is that most do not realize the extent of the damage these substances can do to their bodies. Nor do they believe that taking these drugs can land them in jail, mess up their future, or even lead to their death.

Prescription drugs have become so popular that young people have come up with a new name for get-togethers at which they abuse prescription drugs: "pharm parties." This term comes from the word "pharmaceuticals," a fancy name for drugs. A pharm party is often held in a teenager's home, usually when parents are out or away. Friends gather to consume pills, often foolishly adding alcohol into the mix. This may sound like fun, but when the drugs kick in, people's behavior becomes unpredictable, and bad things often happen.

Prescription Drugs Used as "Academic Steroids"

Many teens feel pressure from adults and from their peers to achieve in and outside of school. Similar to athletes who cut corners by taking

Students who are tired or have trouble concentrating are turning to the illegal use of prescription stimulants to help them study.

steroids to make them stronger or faster, a growing number of young people are improperly using prescription drugs as "academic steroids." These drugs, including the stimulants Ritalin and Adderall, enable students to concentrate for long periods for tests or pull all-nighters in order to hand in final papers on time. Similar to strong coffee, these drugs can give you the energy you need to make it through a sleepless night or a tiring day. This isn't the end of the story, however.

Teens who take the drugs say they get a buzzing sensation at first, then their mouths dry out, and sometimes they lose their appetite. Some become addicted to the feelings the drugs give them. Others find they need greater and greater amounts of the drugs to feel as though they are getting the same benefits they used to. We'll look at stimulants more closely in chapter 4.

Legal Drugs Used Illegally

A big problem with prescription drug abuse is that of public perception, or the way people view them. You are probably familiar with stories in the news or from your personal life of teenagers who have fallen victim to illegal drug abuse. No doubt, your parents, the media, teachers, and friends have warned you about cocaine, heroin, methamphetamine, and other dangerous illegal drugs.

Prescription drugs are all around you, too. Hardly a day goes by that you don't read a newspaper headline or see an advertisement for a new "miracle" pill that cures one ailment or another. You may believe that because some of your friends are on Prozac, Ritalin, Xanax, or another drug, there is little harm in experimenting with these. But you're wrong—maybe dead wrong.

"We Know We'll Get Pills"

One reason prescription drug abuse is on the rise is that pills are often easier to use than illegal drugs. Obtaining and using cocaine or marijuana can be a complicated and dangerous process compared to getting prescription drugs. For some teens, pills are no further away than a parent's medicine cabinet. And it takes only a second to pop a pill.

Students are buying, selling, and trading pills in colleges, high schools, and even junior high schools. The National Center on Addiction and Substance Abuse reported that about 2.3 million Americans between the ages of twelve and seventeen took prescription medications illegally in 2003. The number has only grown since then.

Medical professionals routinely prescribe medication for pain or to recover from medical procedures. These pills often end up in the hands of young people who abuse them. One anonymous female high school student told *Time* magazine, "We rejoice when someone has a medical thing, like, gets their wisdom teeth out or has back pain, because we know we'll get pills." Some students steal such medications from their friends or from school nurses' offices; others obtain them through suspicious Internet pharmacies. Not surprisingly, teens have come up with their own word for stealing pills: "pharming."

It doesn't matter why you improperly use prescription drugs, whether it's for fun, to study longer, to self-medicate, or for the misguided aim of "gaining experience." Whatever the reason, the unauthorized use of such substances can be a prescription for disaster. Don't think something bad can happen to you? *USA Today* reported in June 2006 that about one-quarter of the 1.3 million drug-related emergency room visits involved prescription medication and over-the-counter drugs. It's a good bet that most of those people didn't think they'd have a problem either.

In many homes, a wide selection of prescription drugs is no further away than the medicine cabinet. Easy availability is a big part of the prescription drug abuse problem.

Types of Prescription Drugs

Before we get into the incredibly disgusting story of how these drugs affect your mind and body, you should understand what these drugs are and what their legitimate purposes are. The most commonly abused prescription drugs can be classified in one of three groups: opioid painkillers, depressants, and stimulants.

The Internet has made it easy to refill prescriptions. Online pharmacies will deliver pills right to your house.

Opioid Painkillers

Opioids are generally prescribed to help someone suffering from pain, whether it is chronic pain (constant, long-term pain) or temporary pain from a medical procedure or illness. Commonly abused painkillers include OxyContin, Vicodin, and Demerol.

Central Nervous System Depressants: “Downers”

A second class of prescription drugs is used to treat sleep disorders, anxiety, and panic attacks. These are called central nervous system depressants, or downers. Two popular ones are Valium and Xanax. Both of these prescription medications are highly addictive if abused.

Central Nervous System Stimulants: "Uppers"

A third class of commonly abused prescription drugs is central nervous system stimulants, or uppers. Their effect on the body is not too different from that of cocaine or methamphetamines. Of the drugs in this group, Ritalin is perhaps the most widely used and most likely to be illegally distributed. Other popular ones are Dexedrine and Adderall.

Mixing and Matching

A major problem with prescription drug abuse is mixing and matching drugs. When you are young, it's natural to be adventurous. At pharm parties, abusers regularly mix prescription drugs with alcohol and with street drugs. Friends often gather and exchange pills, many times not knowing what the pills are for. This can result in dangerous and deadly drug cocktails that do serious and permanent damage to your body and brain.

2

Opioid Painkillers

Opioid painkillers are also known as narcotic analgesics. This means they are painkillers ("analgesic") that can put you into a daze or stupor ("narcotic"). For those suffering from chronic or temporary discomfort, proper doses of opioid painkillers make life bearable. The problem begins when these painkillers fall into the wrong hands. If you use prescription painkillers without really needing them, you can cause yourself a lot more pain in the long run than you bargained for.

Opioids are synthetic (human-made) drugs that are chemically similar to opium. (Yes, this is the same plant that produces heroin, the dangerous and super-addictive drug.) Examples of opioids include morphine and codeine. Two other popular painkillers are hydrocodone and oxycodone. These generic drugs are better known by their trade names, Vicodin and OxyContin, respectively.

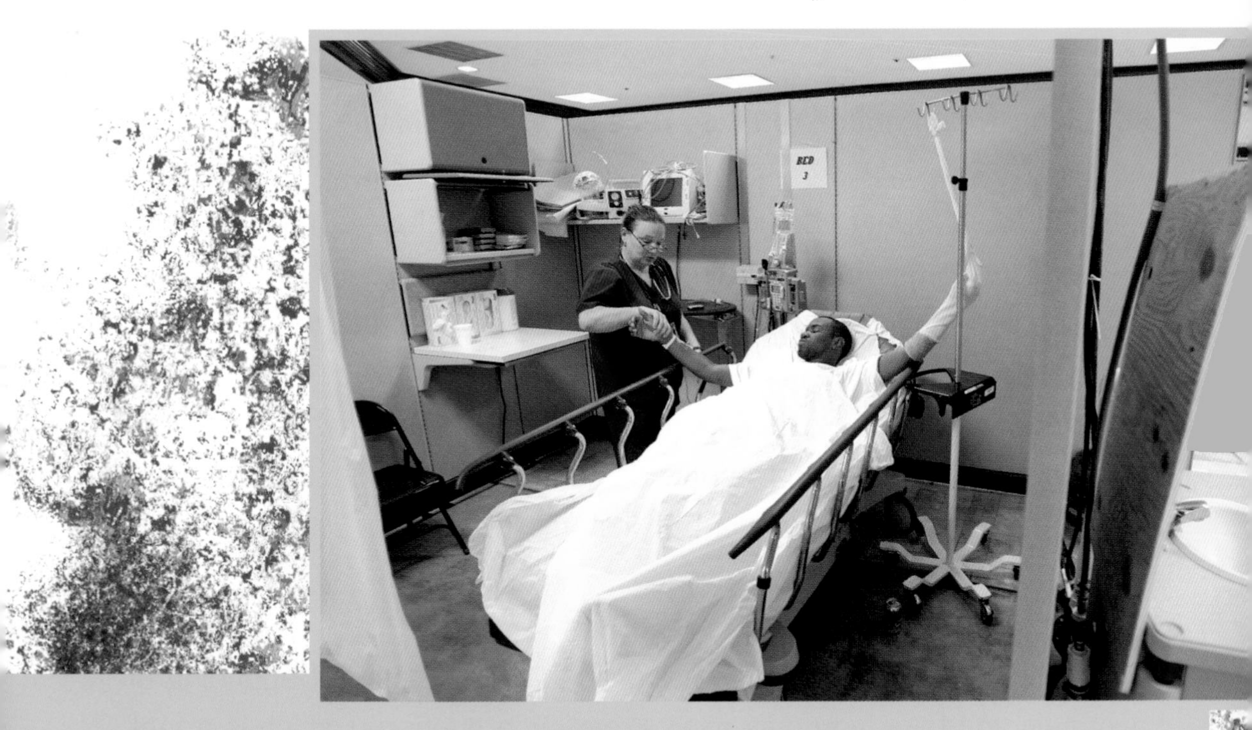

This unfortunate emergency room patient broke his arm. In such situations, opioid painkillers provide much needed temporary relief.

How Do Opioids Work?

Knowing how opioids work helps you understand why they are so easy to abuse. Opioids attach to opioid receptors—tiny regions found in cells throughout the nervous system. (Your nervous system is made up of the body parts that control your behavior and allow you to see and experience the world, feel happy or sad, and feel pain or pleasure.) When opioids in your bloodstream attach to these receptors, they change the way you feel pain.

Opioids also affect chemicals in the brain that change the way you feel pleasure. In the human brain, there are billions of cells called neurons that send information to and receive information from the rest of your body. Chemicals that help pass along information between the neurons are called neurotransmitters. One of these is dopamine, which controls the sensation of pleasure. The opioids hydrocodone and oxycodone greatly affect the normal amount of dopamine in your brain.

Looking for a Good Time?

When you first take an opioid, you'll probably feel happier. Depending on how much you take, you may even experience euphoria, which is a feeling of extreme happiness. Taking a prescribed amount of a painkiller when you really need it usually doesn't create an intense feeling. Still, if you have ever had a tooth pulled or some other medical procedure, you may have felt funny or a little giggly when you took the pills the doctor gave you for the pain.

Some users say they take painkillers to reduce the stress in their daily lives. Many others take them recreationally because they are cheaper and work faster than alcohol. Even worse, some recreational users take painkillers along with alcohol, claiming that this gets them drunk quicker. Separately, drinking too much and popping Vicodin are bad ideas. Imagine putting the two together!

Opioids and Your Body

Because opioids are designed to dull pain, they slow down your body. A little too much of an opioid like Vicodin or OxyContin produces symptoms that include cold, clammy skin; excessive sweating; dry mouth; nausea, dizziness or feeling lightheaded; and sleepiness or tiredness.

But you'd be lucky getting off so easily. Too much of an opioid can be lethal. Do slow breathing, extreme weakness, and dizziness sound like a good time to you? How do you like the feeling of your throat closing, leaving you unable to breathe? Opioids can induce seizures or blackouts. By themselves or combined with alcohol or other pills, painkillers not only kill pain, they can also kill you.

Dangerous Cocktails

Mark Bauer was an eighteen-year-old high school student and weight lifter from York, Pennsylvania. He started self-medicating with prescription painkillers because of back pain he had suffered from working out so much. Mark's father,

Opioids can have the same effects as their distant cousin, the illegal narcotic heroin. They can cause blackouts, overdoses, and even death.

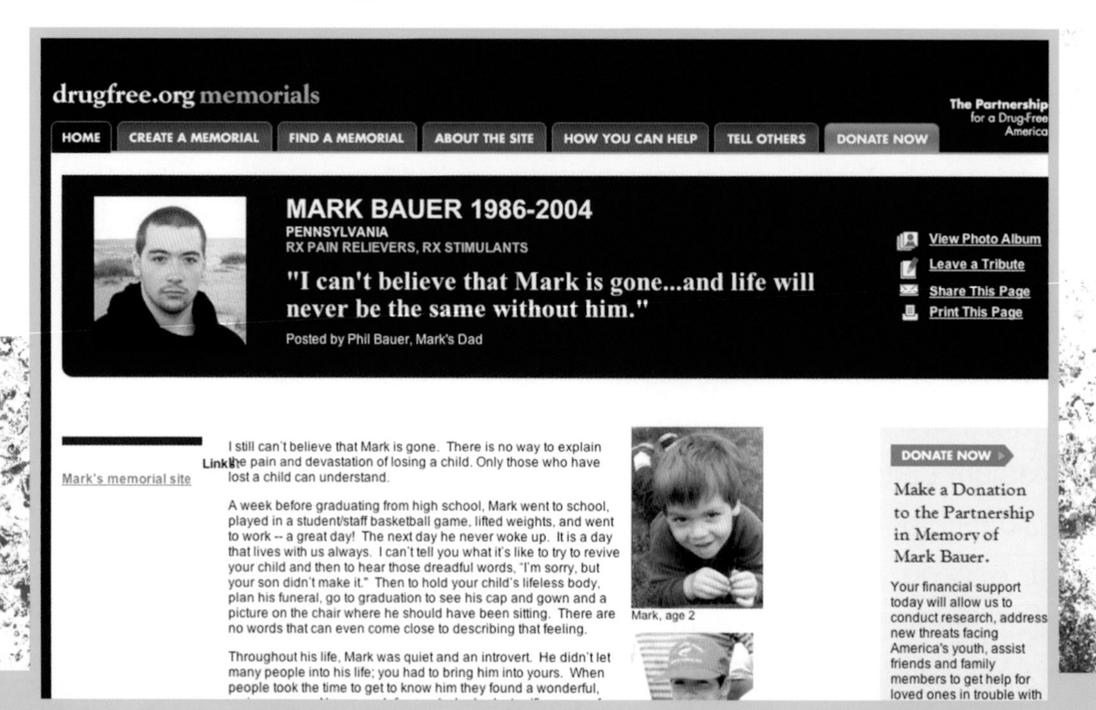

The Web site Drugfree.org posted this online memorial page for teen Mark Bauer. He died by overdosing on a dangerous mixture of prescription drugs.

Phil Bauer, is still grieving for his son: Mark died of an overdose in May 2004. Doctors found that Mark's blood had traces of morphine, OxyContin, and acetaminophen. Acetaminophen is found in Tylenol, but it's also in the prescription drugs Vicodin and Percocet.

Mark's case reflects one of the serious problems stemming from the explosion of prescription drug abuse. Namely, no one can really tell how a particular combination of drugs, plus alcohol and illegal drugs, may affect a person. Scientists and doctors have a great deal of knowledge about how to treat heroin and cocaine addicts who have overdosed, but the same is not true for victims coming from pharm parties. Picture a young person bringing a friend to the emergency room. The patient's eyes are rolled back in his head, his breathing is irregular, and his skin is pale, cold, and clammy. He is not responding to voices. Then the doctors find that the person who brought him doesn't have a clue as to which drugs or how much of each drug was consumed. How are they supposed to start treating the patient?

Oxycodone/OxyContin

Some readers may be familiar with the story of talk show host Rush Limbaugh and his very public struggle with abusing the prescription medication OxyContin. The scientific name for the drug is actually oxycodone. People usually take it to reduce the effects of moderate or severe pain. Popular oxycodone-based prescription drugs include Percodan and Percocet, as well as OxyContin.

Oxycodone shares some negative side effects with Valium, including weakness and dizziness. More serious side effects include cold and clammy skin, slowed or difficult breathing, seizures, and unconsciousness. Lesser side effects can be a huge pain, too. Are you ready for dry mouth, nausea, throwing up, and losing your appetite? You may also get tired or lightheaded. As a bonus, some patients have muscle twitches and trouble urinating and defecating (going to the bathroom).

If someone has the following symptoms while doing OxyContin for fun, he or she may be overdosing: slowed breathing, dizziness, weakness, cold and clammy skin, and loss of consciousness. In more serious overdoses, oxycodone may cause seizures and even coma. You can sometimes tell an OxyContin overdose case by the person's eyes: the pupils tend to dilate, or get very small, like pinholes.

Snorting Pills

OxyContin tablets are supposed to be taken orally (by mouth), and they are formulated to be "controlled-release." In other words, the pill is made so that your body absorbs the drug slowly over time. But many OxyContin abusers don't swallow the pill. Instead, they crush it up and snort it. This way, the drug is absorbed through the mucous membranes in the nose. Snorting the drugs hits a user harder than it is supposed to—way harder.

Paul Michaud, an eighteen-year-old from Boston, Massachusetts, discovered this the hard way. Paul talked to *USA Today* in June 2006. He said he had started taking OxyContin because it relaxed him and helped him escape from emotional pain. His father had just died, and he was depressed. Paul eventually was snorting up to five high-strength pills a day. As of the writing of the article, the young man was in his fourth month of a yearlong drug treatment program.

Injecting Pills

Snorting pills is bad enough, but some hard-core OxyContin abusers dissolve the crushed tablets in water and shoot the mixture directly into their muscles or veins. Using needles for drugs is never a good idea. Sharing needles or using dirty needles can spread life-threatening blood-transmitted

Doctors and nurses rush to treat a patient who overdosed. The hospital emergency room is a common destination for opioid abusers.

diseases like HIV and hepatitis. In addition, injecting drugs can cause serious infections, abscesses, and even gangrene. Shooting OxyContin into your veins can block small blood vessels, as there are tiny particles in the pills that do not dissolve in water. A blocked blood vessel can rupture, or break, and cause internal bleeding. Blockages can prevent the delivery of blood into your lungs, or to the retinas of your eyes. Imagine going blind or having trouble breathing for the rest of your life, just for a temporary high.

A young abuser prepares a hypodermic needle for shooting up drugs. Using needles is dangerous for many reasons: blood-transmitted diseases, infections, and overdose.

Kicking the Habit

Getting addicted to an opioid like OxyContin can be frighteningly easy. Breaking an addiction is anything but. National Public Radio interviewed Ryan, a seventeen-year-old high school senior from Tewsbury, Massachusetts. He tried OxyContin at a party when he was sixteen and found that he preferred it to marijuana, which left him "weirded out." He started using OxyContin every day and soon realized he felt sick if he skipped a day. Eventually, he ended up in bed, withdrawing from OxyContin. "It was like somebody was inside of your head with a hammer," he told NPR. "You feel like you're going to die . . . just laying there in the bed, sweat pouring off of you . . . Then, five minutes later, you're freezing . . . then you'd be throwing up . . . I was sick as a dog and . . . I couldn't believe it. I was actually scared," he admitted.

3

Depressants, or Downers

The prescription drugs known as downers are chemically different from painkillers. Medically, downers are better known as central nervous system (CNS) depressants. These substances typically slow down normal brain activity, though they may act on several parts of the body. In large doses, some powerful depressants are used as general anesthetics. In other words, this is the stuff that knocks you out and keeps you from feeling pain during a major medical procedure.

Doctors prescribe CNS depressants to treat patients suffering from anxiety, nervousness, panic attacks, stress, and sleeplessness. Like painkillers, depressants have been the subject of great concern for medical experts, educators, parents, and legal authorities. That's because they recently have become popular party drugs—a cheap, quick way for teens to get high (or, more precisely, low).

How Do CNS Depressants Work?

Like painkillers, CNS depressants work by changing the user's brain chemicals. Depressants affect the neurotransmitter gamma-aminobutyric acid (GABA). GABA decreases brain activity. While there are differences among them, most depressants work by increasing the amount of GABA. The desired effect is to calm the mind, especially for people who are anxious or cannot sleep.

CNS depressants fall into two categories: barbiturates and benzodiazepines. Barbiturates were popular years ago. Nowadays, benzodiazepines are more widely prescribed, mainly because they have a lower risk of overdose. Some famous people (and even more non-famous people) have died of barbiturate overdoses. These people included starlet Marilyn Monroe and guitarist Jimi Hendrix. Today, barbiturates are mainly used as medication for those who cannot take benzodiazepines because of the risk of seizures.

Benzodiazepines may be less potent than barbiturates, but they can be perilous in other ways. Benzodiazepines are highly addictive, and getting off of them can cause severe withdrawal symptoms. This is especially true for those quitting "cold turkey," or trying to give them up suddenly and completely. With depressants, which work by slowing brain activity, sudden withdrawal can be quite dangerous. Without the drugs, the brain's activity may increase very quickly. This uncontrolled brain activity can lead to convulsions or seizures. Those who are dependent on

Jimi Hendrix, considered to be one of the greatest rock guitarists of all time, died from an overdose of downers. He was only twenty-seven years old.

depressants should consult a physician before trying to quit.

All the Way Down

For those who are not diagnosed with anxiety or some other disorder, taking depressants can be an express ticket to the emergency room—or the cemetery. Two of the most widely abused depressants are benzodiazepines. One is diazepam, more commonly known by its trade name, Valium. The other is alprazolam, better known by the trade name Xanax. Both drugs pop up at countless pharm parties.

Valium: The Chill Pill

Diazepam is one of the most common drugs in use today. The World Health Organization lists it as one of the core medications that a nation or hospital system must have to meet minimum requirements for medical care. Doctors prescribe it for anxiety, insomnia (sleeplessness), seizures, muscle problems, and as an aid for alcoholics who are having withdrawal symptoms. Some sources report that 30 million Americans (one in ten!) use Valium. Sixty million Valium prescriptions are filled out annually in the United States.

Again, it is when Valium falls into the wrong hands—kids looking for a good time, or those who are self-medicating—that things go wrong. Under normal circumstances, depressants like Valium increase GABA levels in the brain to a normal level, allowing the patient to relax just enough. A Valium abuser, on the other hand, usually takes much more than is safe. In this case, GABA levels can increase to the point that a person's heart rate and breathing slow down enough to cause death.

Valium: Side Effects and Overdose

Users of Valium, even those with a prescription, risk some pretty gross side effects. Some people experience a yellowing of the eyes and skin. You can get sores in the mouth or in your throat, or a rash. Others may experience hallucinations (seeing and hearing things that aren't really there), or they may become extremely confused. Other side effects include nausea, vomiting, diarrhea, or constipation (inability to go to the bathroom). If those don't sound bad enough, a Valium overdose is worse. Short of a huge overdose, which can lead to death, too much Valium can make you intensely sleepy, dizzy, or confused. As with many depressants, if you take too much, you might have trouble walking, talking, and breathing.

Xanax

Alprazolam is another benzodiazepine that has become popular among prescription drug abusers. It is marketed widely under the trade name Xanax. Studies show that, under normal circumstances, Xanax works very well in treating such psychological problems as panic disorder and panic attacks, long-term severe anxiety disorder, and depression.

For those who use Xanax as prescribed, side effects may include sleepiness, confusion, tiredness, dizziness, and headaches. Many users experience a temporary period of intense happiness (euphoria) when first taking Xanax. This sensation disappears over time, in most cases.

Medical professionals agree that alprazolam has high potential for misuse and dependence. It's also one of the more potent forms of benzodiazepine, making it difficult to stop using completely. If you quit using Xanax, withdrawal symptoms may include nervousness, panic attacks, muscle cramps, and seizures. These symptoms can be severe, so patients coming off Xanax usually need to decrease their intake over a period of weeks, or even months.

Some drug users take Xanax to "come down." This means they use it to ease themselves off the high of other drugs, including cocaine, ecstasy (MDMA), hallucinogens such as LSD, or prescription stimulants like Ritalin. As you know by now, this combining of drugs can be extremely dangerous.

4 Stimulants, or Uppers

Stimulants are popular and commonly abused drugs. Illegal use of stimulants like speed (Benzedrine) and crystal meth (methamphetamine) has grown in recent years. But the abuse of legal prescription stimulants is exploding, too.

You may consider a stimulant such as Ritalin (the trade name of methylphenidate) as a part of your normal landscape. But an overdose of Ritalin is no less dangerous than overdosing on cocaine. In fact, Ritalin is classified as a Schedule II substance. This means that the U.S. government understands that Ritalin has a legitimate medical purpose, but it also recognizes that it is very easy to abuse and become addicted to.

Prescription Stimulants

The number of prescriptions written for stimulants such as Ritalin and Adderall has skyrocketed in the past two decades. Ritalin has long been used to treat attention

Stimulants can help children diagnosed with ADHD, who sometimes have too much energy. Nine-year-old Marty *(above)* takes Ritalin to control his behavior.

deficit disorder (ADD) and attention-deficit/hyperactivity disorder (ADHD). The drug can also help in treating narcolepsy, a condition in which the patient can't help falling asleep.

Many experts question whether all of those who are diagnosed with ADHD actually need medication. Regardless, millions of Americans, mostly young people, have legal prescriptions for stimulants to treat ADHD. What exactly is ADHD anyway?

Attention-deficit/hyperactivity disorder can include many symptoms. Generally, it is used to describe children and teenagers who have a great deal of trouble paying attention. They may also have too much energy, acting out with disruptive behavior that makes it hard for them to relate to other children or their own families. For them, stimulants can be a miracle cure. But many young people are using Ritalin and Adderall for all the wrong reasons: to get high, lose weight, or help them stay up all night to study.

How Do Stimulants Work?

Stimulants like Ritalin are designed to affect monoamines, which are neurotransmitters in your brain. Taking stimulants increases the presence of monoamines. As a result, your blood pressure and heart rate increase. Also, blood vessels constrict (get smaller), blood sugar increases, and breathing rate increases. Stimulants increase the presence of a particular monoamine, dopamine, which controls our sensation of pleasure. That's why users of stimulants often feel euphoria.

Medical professionals are not exactly sure why stimulants calm down people with ADHD. But one thing is clear: for stimulant abusers, drugs like Ritalin do the exact opposite of calming people down.

What Stimulant Abuse Can Do

The preferred method of delivery for many abusers of Ritalin is through the nose. They crush the pills into a fine powder and inhale it. Some observers have labeled Ritalin "kiddie cocaine," since so many young people have tried it in this manner. The drug is absorbed through the nose's mucous membranes, and it hits the brain and body more quickly. Usually, abusers take far more of the drug than those who use it in safe dosages.

Snorting any drug can lead to irreversible damage to the nose. Prolonged inhalation of powdered drugs dries out the mucous membranes, cracking this delicate part of the body. Nosebleeds are a common hazard. In addition, you could have trouble breathing normally, and your sense of smell could be permanently impaired. Have you ever felt the soft material that makes up your nose? It's called cartilage, and it forms the septum, the part of your nose separating your nostrils. Over time, repeated use of powdered drugs damages your septum and creates a hole between your nasal passages!

Too much Ritalin can give you an irregular heartbeat, which can be scary. Your body temperature may become dangerously high. Your cardiovascular system (heart and blood vessels) may fail, or you may have a seizure. Some abusers who take a great deal of Ritalin in a short time report feeling very angry and hostile. Others who take the drug over a long period say they often feel paranoid, as though "people are out to get them." Because of these dangers, the U.S. Drug Enforcement Administration (DEA) lists Ritalin as a "drug of concern." As a stimulant, it is more powerful than caffeine but not quite as powerful as, say, amphetamines. But it can be as dangerous, especially the way it's being abused nowadays.

Ritalin and Alcohol: A Dangerous Mix

One of the most foolish things someone can do at a party is mix alcohol with prescription medications. What is ironic is that some fun-seeking teens don't just use Ritalin to "boost" a drunken good time, but they actually take it to help them drink more. They think they feel less drunk, but in reality, they are just as drunk and in even greater danger of alcohol poisoning or Ritalin overdose.

Ritalin: The Study Drug

Many who take Ritalin illegally do it for fun. It makes them feel pretty good. But Ritalin abuse can result even when someone has good intentions—like studying hard to get that A on an exam. According to many reports, college and high school students regularly use Ritalin to stay awake to study. With the help of the drug, they can maintain abnormally high levels of concentration.

Nora Volkow, director of the National Institute on Drug Abuse (NIDA), said that students hoping to excel were playing a dangerous game. She told the *Washington Post* in February 2006 that young people taking prescription drugs to study were "playing roulette." She continued, "If you get addicted, you will not only not get into Harvard, you will not finish high school." Sadly, the same article told of a father visiting his son's college fraternity. He was swamped by requests for Adderall prescriptions by his son's fraternity brothers, who were hoping to improve their academic performance.

5 A National Crisis

Between 1999 and 2004, the leading cause of accidental death in the United States was automobile crashes. For years, the second-leading cause was fatal injuries from falls. But by 2004, drug overdoses had taken over the number-two spot. The Centers for Disease Control and Prevention (CDC) reported in February 2007 that 11,155 people fatally overdosed on drugs in 1999. In 2004, that number had risen to 19,838.

The Prescription Drug Problem Grows

In 2006, the National Institute on Drug Abuse (NIDA) published a report based on information gathered from the Drug Abuse Warning Network (DAWN). NIDA said that for the year 2004, Valium and OxyContin were among the most commonly abused drugs. DAWN estimated that 495,732 visits to hospital emergency rooms involved prescription or over-the-counter drug abuse.

Benzodiazepines such as Valium accounted for 144,385 cases; opioid pain relievers such as OxyContin accounted for 132,207 cases. Even scarier, 57 percent of such emergency room visits were for patients who had taken multiple drugs. Based on its research, NIDA estimated that as many as 9 million Americans of all ages abuse prescription drugs annually.

Drug abuse and related deaths, once seen as inner-city problems, have spread to the suburbs and rural areas with lightning speed. Even small towns in the South have seen an explosion in drug use and crime. For example, Tazewell, Virginia, was a sleepy and safe place fifteen years ago. But OxyContin flooded the area in the 1990s. Most of the prescriptions were written out to disabled or retired coal miners dealing with chronic pain. Now Tazewell, a town of 4,100 inhabitants, has 1,100 people on probation. Most of these folks were arrested for illegally dealing OxyContin, or for committing robbery or burglary to get money for the drug.

Dependence, Tolerance, and Withdrawal

As the case of Tazewell, Virginia, shows, even people who take painkillers for legitimate reasons can become dependent on them. Long-term use of opioids can lead to a physical dependence, which means that the body becomes used to having a certain substance in it and reacts badly if that substance is suddenly taken away. This reaction is called withdrawal, and it happens to those with a dependence on a wide variety of stuff: alcohol, cocaine, heroin, and—you guessed it—prescription drugs.

The physical effects of withdrawal from prescription drugs are not pleasant. For example, if you are dependent on OxyContin and you suddenly stop using it, your withdrawal symptoms may include restlessness, enlarged pupils, watery eyes, runny nose, sweating, chills, and muscle aches. More severe cases may also involve irritability, anxiety, joint pain, weakness, cramps, insomnia, nausea, vomiting, diarrhea, rapid breathing, and a fast heart rate. Fortunately, there's one way to make sure you never have to suffer these symptoms: don't abuse prescription painkillers!

Dependence often goes hand in hand with tolerance. A person develops tolerance when his or her body needs more of the drug to get the same results from it. If you are taking Vicodin or OxyContin regularly, the rush you felt the first week or so of doing it eventually decreases. Soon, you have to swallow or crush up and snort more of these drugs to get the same high. You may entertain the idea of injecting the drugs to get an intense high. At the same time, you start to need the drug just to feel normal.

Addiction: How Can You Tell?

Dependence and addiction are not quite the same thing. Addiction occurs when a person has no control and will try to get the drug no matter what the cost. An addict does this in spite of knowing the negative effects of the drug. Often, these negative effects are both physical and mental.

One of the great obstacles for parents, friends, and teachers who want to help teens who are abusing prescription drugs is that it's often difficult to tell that there is a problem. Phil Bauer said of his dead son, Mark: "He wasn't hanging out all night . . . We didn't see a bleary-eyed guy. He wasn't slurring his words."

Treatment: A Light at the End of the Tunnel?

Despite the lives that prescription drug use has taken or ruined, there is hope. If someone has a serious problem with prescription drugs, a treatment program can be the best help. This is especially true for those taking certain prescription medications that have severe withdrawal effects if one stops taking them cold turkey. The most effective drug treatment depends on the drugs and on the individual person. There is no one way that works for everyone.

For many abusers of opioid painkillers, methadone (used to treat heroin addiction) may be helpful. For treating stimulant addiction, on the other hand, there are no proven medications. When helping someone kick an addiction to stimulants, doctors often employ techniques developed over the years to treat cocaine and methamphetamine addicts. Treatment for people addicted to CNS depressants varies as well. For them, the situation is usually more complicated because many depressant abusers are also hooked on alcohol or other drugs.

An early and crucial aspect of drug treatment is detoxification, or detox. This is a process that rids the patient's body of drugs and helps the person deal with the physical problems of withdrawal. Going into detox is the first step in a long road for many addicts.

A counselor listens as a recovering abuser relates her experience. Such group counseling can be invaluable for teens recovering from prescription drug abuse.

While the physical need for a drug may no longer exist, the psychological need for a drug may persist. This is why ongoing counseling, especially in the form of a support group, is a necessary part of "staying clean," or drug-free. Narcotics Anonymous (NA) meetings, where addicts come together and support each other on the road to recovery, have helped millions. Family counseling helps to reconnect people with loved ones they may have alienated during their addiction.

In Conclusion: No Easy Answer

The problem of prescription drug abuse has no easy answers. In fact, it is looking for the easy answer, the quick high, that gets many into trouble in the first place. As pharmaceutical companies continue to make billions of dollars by creating new drugs, it is unlikely that the issue of prescription drug abuse will go away anytime soon. In the end, it is up to you to make smart decisions to avoid the incredibly disgusting consequences of prescription drug abuse.

Glossary

addiction Compulsive need for and use of a substance, even when it causes great harm.

analgesic Drug used to relieve pain.

attention deficit disorder (ADD) Condition that leaves a person unable to focus on one thing at a time.

attention-deficit/hyperactivity disorder (ADHD) ADD with the additional problem of overactive and often socially unacceptable behavior.

benzodiazepine Type of central nervous system depressant usually prescribed to help a person sleep or relax.

central nervous system (CNS) Body system made up of the brain and spinal cord; the CNS regulates behavior, movement, emotions, mental faculties, and the senses.

central nervous system depressants Medications that slow down body functions; typically used to treat anxiety, nervousness, panic attacks, stress, and sleeplessness.

dependence Condition where the body needs a certain substance in order to function.

detoxification Also known as detox; a crucial step of a person's treatment for substance abuse, in which the body is cleansed of the addictive substance.

dopamine A brain chemical that regulates emotion, motivation, and movement.

gamma-aminobutyric acid (GABA) A neurotransmitter that slows brain activity; many CNS depressants work by increasing GABA amounts in the brain.

monoamines Neurotransmitters that help regulate various bodily functions, including blood sugar levels, the respiratory system, and the experience of pleasure.

neurotransmitters Chemicals that help send information between the brain's nerve cells, or neurons.

opioids Family of prescription drugs that are designed to relieve pain.

over-the-counter Describes medications that do not require a prescription from a medical professional.

Ritalin Commercial name for methylphenidate, a stimulant widely prescribed to treat ADD and ADHD.

side effects Unintended, typically negative effects of a medication.

stimulants Drugs that increase the activity of the central nervous system.

tolerance Capacity of the body to become less responsive to a drug or other substance.

Valium Commercial name for one of the main brands of diazepam, a popular CNS depressant.

Vicodin Commercial name for the most widely known form of hydrocodone, a popular prescription opioid.

withdrawal Physical and mental effects that occur when a person stops using a drug on which he or she has a dependence.

Xanax Commercial name for the most popular brand of alprazolam, a CNS depressant.

For More Information

Narcotics Anonymous
P.O. Box 9999
Van Nuys, CA 91409
(818) 773-9999
Web site: http://www.na.org

National Institute on Drug Abuse (NIDA)
6001 Executive Boulevard, Room 5213
Bethesda, MD 20892
(301) 443-1124
Web sites: http://www.nida.nih.gov; http://www.drugabuse.gov

Pharmaceutical Research and Manufacturers of America (PhRMA)
950 F Street NW, Suite 300
Washington, DC 20004
(202) 835-3400
Web site: http://www.phrma.org

Substance Abuse and Mental Health Services Administration (SAMHSA)
Center for Substance Abuse Treatment
5600 Fishers Lane, Suite 618

Rockwall II
Rockville, MD 20857
(301) 443-5052
Web site: http://www.samhsa.gov

White House Office on National Drug Control Policy
Drug Policy Information Clearinghouse
P.O. Box 6000
Rockville, MD 20849
(800) 666-3332
Web site: http://www.whitehousedrugpolicy.gov

Web Sites

Due to the changing nature of Internet links, Rosen Publishing has developed an online list of Web sites related to the subject of this book. This site is updated regularly. Please use this link to access the list:

http://www.rosenlinks.com/idd/abpd

For Further Reading

Aretha, David. *Methamphetamine and Amphetamines* (Drugs). Berkeley Heights, NJ: Enslow Publishers, Inc., 2005.

Fitzhugh, Karla. *Prescription Drug Abuse (What's the Deal?)*. Portsmouth, NH: Heinemann, 2005.

Hiber, Amanda, ed. *Are Americans Overmedicated?* (At Issue Series). Farmington Hills, MI: Greenhaven Press, 2006.

Murphy, Patricia J. *Avoiding Drugs* (Pull Ahead Books). Minneapolis, MN: Lerner Publishing, 2005.

Olive, M. Foster. *Prescription Pain Relievers* (Drugs: The Straight Facts Series). New York, NY: Chelsea House Publishers, 2004.

Ragon, Bruce, John Haley, and Mark J. Kittleson, general ed. *The Truth About Drugs*. New York, NY: Facts on File, 2005.

Rebman, Renee C. *Addictions and Risky Behaviors: Cutting, Bingeing, Snorting, and Other Dangers* (Issues in Focus Today). Berkeley Heights, NJ: Enslow Publishers, Inc., 2006.

Schwartzenberger, Tina. *Substance Use and Abuse* (Understanding Global Issues). New York, NY: Weigl Publishers, 2004.

Toufexis, Donna, Sayamwong E. Hammack, and David J. Triggle, consulting ed. *Anti-Anxiety Drugs* (Drugs: The Straight Facts Series). New York, NY: Chelsea House Publishers, 2006.

Watkins, Christine, ed. *At Issue: Prescription Drugs*. Farmington Hills, MI: Greenhaven Press, 2006.

Bibliography

Arnold, Chris. "Teen Abuse of Painkiller OxyContin on the Rise." National Public Radio's "All Things Considered." December 15, 2005. Retrieved December 2005 (http://www.npr.org/templates/story/story.php?storyId=5061674).

Banta, Carolyn. "Trading for a High." Time. July 24, 2005. Retrieved January 2007 (http://www.time.com/time/magazine/article/0,9171,1086173,00.html).

Bowman, Rex. "Prescription for Crime." Time. March 21, 2005. Retrieved December 2006 (http://www.time.com/time/magazine/article/0,9171,1039712,00.html).

Childs, Dan. "Access to Legal Drugs Fueling Teen Drug Culture." ABC News. December 21, 2006. Retrieved January 2007 (http://i.abcnews.com/Health/Drugs/story?id=2743870&page=1).

Harris, Gardiner. "Proof Is Scant on Psychiatric Drug Mix for Young." New York Times. November 23, 2006. Retrieved January 2007 (http://www.nytimes.com/2006/11/23/health/23kids.html?hp&ex=1164344400&en=266fbd110aa0d9cf&ei=5094&partner=homepage).

Kalb, Claudia. "Playing with Pain Killers." *Newsweek*. April 9, 2001.

Kluger, Jeffrey. "Medicating Young Minds." Time. November 3, 2003. Retrieved January 2007 (http://www.time.com/time/magazine/article/0,9171,1006034,00.html).

Leinwand, Donna. "Prescription Abusers Not Just After a High." USA Today. May 5, 2005. Retrieved January 2007 (http://www.usatoday.com/news/health/2005-05-25-drugs_x.htm).

Leinwand, Donna. "Prescription Drugs Find Place in Teen Culture." USA Today. June 12, 2006. Retrieved January 2007 (http://www.usatoday.com/news/health/2006-06-12-teens-pharm-drugs_x.htm?csp=34).

Marks, Alexandra. "Teen Drug Abuse Moves to the Medicine Cabinet." Christian Science Monitor. December 22, 2006. Retrieved December 2006 (http://www.csmonitor.com/2006/1222/p02s01-ussc.html).

Rubin, Rita. "Opioids Help Patients, but Are a Conflict for Doctors." USA Today. August 9, 2001. Retrieved December 2006 (http://www.usatoday.com/news/health/2001-08-09-opioids.htm#more).

Stobbe, Mike. "CDC: Dramatic Rise in Drug Deaths." Time. February 9, 2007. Retrieved February 2007 (http://www.time.com/time/health/article/0,8599,1587950,00.html).

Vedantam, Shankar. "Millions Have Misused ADHD Stimulant Drugs, Study Says." Washington Post. February 24, 2006. Retrieved January 2007 (http://seattletimes.nwsource.com/html/nationworld/2002827352_webadhd24.html).

Index

About the Author

Philip Wolny is a writer, editor, and M.A. student currently residing in Krakow, Poland. He has always been fascinated by the American (and worldwide) dilemma surrounding the use and abuse of both illegal and prescription drugs. He is also happy for those he has known who have persevered and defeated the specter of drug abuse in their lives. Wolny has only high hopes for those still struggling.

Photo Credits

Cover, p. 1 © www.istockphoto.com/Jamie Evans; pp. 5, 8 © shutterstock.com; p. 10 © www.istockphoto.com/drflet; p. 13 © Felicia Martinez/PhotoEdit; p. 17 © Robyn Beck/AFP/Getty Images; p. 19 © www.istockphoto.com/Jordan Philips; p. 23 © Larry Mulvehill/Photo Researchers, Inc.; p. 24 © Bruce Preston/Getty Images; p. 27 © Evening Standard/Getty Images; p. 31 © Steve Liss/Time Life Pictures/Getty Images; p. 39 © Mary Kate Denny/PhotoEdit.

Designer: Les Kanturek; **Editor:** Christopher Roberts;
Photo Researcher: Amy Feinberg